£3.95

GW01018742

Pathfinder 4

A CILT series for language teachers

Yes - but will they behave?
Managing the interactive classroom

Susan Halliwell

ci LT

Other titles in the PATHFINDER series:

Recording progress (John Thorogood)
Reading for pleasure in a foreign language (Ann Swarbrick)
Schemes of work (Laurie Kershook)
On target: teaching in the target language (Susan Halliwell and Barry Jones)
Communication re-activated: teaching pupils with learning difficulties
(Bernardette Holmes)

Acknowledgements

In publishing these ideas I am indebted to

Caroline Mortlock for her cartoons
Barry Jones for his contributions and advice
all the PGCE students who have borne my presence in their lessons

and those of my own classes who have confronted me, at times uncomfortably, with some of the harsher realities of the language classroom.

First published 1991
Copyright © 1991 Centre for Information on Language Teaching and Research
ISBN 0 948003 44 8

Cover by Logos Design & Advertising
Printed in Great Britain by Direct Printers Ltd.

Published by Centre for Information on Language Teaching and Research, Regent's College, Inner Circle, Regent's Park, London NW1 4NS.

Contents

Introduction

'I can't possibly do pair-work with that lot, they won't stop talking to each other!'

There is a very narrow line between liveliness and restlessness. As we develop more interactive styles of language teaching which encourage plenty of oral work, simultaneous pair-work, movement round the room, and scope for the pupils' sense of fun and imagination, we are all faced with the question of how to organise events so that the liveliness works **for** learning not against it. Some teachers will be able to rely on their personality and their established authority to carry them through whatever teaching method they adopt. Others will develop a teaching style which moves away from the centrally imposed control of the teacher and sets up more independent learning. Most of us, however, will encounter somewhere in our teaching the kind of restlessness and unco-operativeness which can make any form of foreign language work seem an uphill task and can make oral work in particular seem dispiritingly unrealistic. Under those circumstances it is very tempting to abandon exactly the kind of interactive teaching which in less pressured moments we are quite happy to agree is exactly what the pupils both want and need. Even with basically willing and co-operative classes, language lessons can seem hard work and can border on the frenetic.

The question then is how to organise language lessons so that they offer opportunities for real communication and lively interaction while still maintaining a reasonable working atmosphere for pupils and teachers alike.

The starting point of this short book is simple and is something that teachers know instinctively. We all know that, quite independently of the teacher, some activities calm a class down and others stir them up. By exploring this very simple fact in greater depth and by developing quite deliberate strategies based on the insights it offers, the book suggests how, without losing sight of our ideals,

- we can avoid creating problems unnecessarily;
- we can respond constructively to problems which nonetheless do arise;
- we can reduce, even in a more interactive classroom, the need for the kind of overtly imposed control which demands more energy, will power and charismatic personality than most of us have.

The suggestions here apply whether you are teaching from a textbook or from your own materials, and whether you have basically amenable classes or the kind which only have to be mentioned in the staffroom to produce an almost Pavlovian chorus of groans! The ideas offered are not the only approach to the question of interactive language work and control, nor will they solve everything, but they have helped me and have helped those I have already shared them with. I hope they will help you.

1   Anticipating the effect of an activity

Most of us have heard ourselves say at some time the equivalent of 'OK, if you can't do this sensibly (it's usually something we've spent literally hours preparing!) then we'll have to do something really boring. So get out your exercise books...'

We can take this instinctive response and awareness further. We can **anticipate** the probable effects of certain classroom activities and quite deliberately use that insight to construct a controlled framework for an interactive lesson. There are two key questions, which are interrelated:

Does the activity stir or does it settle?
In what way does it involve the learner?

Does it stir or does it settle?

The terms stir and settle are not intended to carry any overtones of good or bad. 'Stir' can be positive in the sense of waking a class up or it can be negative in the sense of making them restless. 'Settle' similarly can mean that a class calms down or it can mean that they sink into a kind of stupefied boredom.

Exactly what you personally find stirs or settles your classes is a matter of your individual experience, circumstances and style. However, within the variations there is a core of experience common to most of us. If we look at the four skills, for example, most of us will agree that as a general rule oral work stirs, listening and reading usually settle and on most occasions writing settles a class like magic. The type of activity within those skills also makes a difference. So games and competitions, for example, tend to stir. Mechanical routines on the other hand tend to settle.

It helps to make yourself lists like those started on the next page. In the particular lists here activities are described in rather general categories. More specific examples are only noted in brackets. This is because my personal set of teaching activities and the shorthand labels I have for them would not necessarily mean anything to anyone else. However, when you make your own list it is a good idea to be as specific as you can.

You can apply the stir/settle distinction to any typical or regular features of your teaching. Do you, for example, have a set of questions and answers with which you routinely begin lessons? If so, ask yourself whether the classes are more settled or more stirred at the end of the routine than they were at the beginning.

teacher/pupil oral work (question/
    answer, checking exercises,
    repetition etc)

competitions (blackboard 'oxo', lotto,
    find me a ..., team games etc)

games (guess what I've got on my
    flashcard/in my hand/on OHP,
    battleships, pelmanism reading
    game etc)

pupil/pupil oral work (dialogues,
    sondages, drills etc)

acting
pair-work ... ?
just listening ... ?

- - - -
- - - -

copying (particularly from a book)
drawing / labelling / colouring
listening WITH SOMETHING TO DO
(grids, tick which one you hear,
find the word, arrange the
sequence, draw what I
describe etc)
being read to / being told a story
watching a video
reading alone
some pair-work ... ?
- - - -
- - - -
- - - -

In fact, in reading the above lists or in writing your own and perhaps discussing them with other teachers, you will have already discovered that there is not a tidy distinction between the two categories. You will probably have found yourself thinking something like '*X works as a settler, but only if...*' or '*Yes, but sometimes...*'. There is obviously another factor at work. Pair-work shows this particularly well. It can lead to noisy inattentive classes or it can lead to classes which are still fairly noisy but in a busy absorbed way. What makes the difference is the degree and nature of involvement which the activity demands or offers.

How does the activity involve the learners?

We can distinguish, although not separate completely, those activities which engage the emotions or the mind and those which occupy the learners physically.

MENTAL ENGAGEMENT

Games, for example, engage the learners' minds by appealing to their sense of fun or their appetite for competition. So, for different reasons, do things they have to work out, like logical puzzles or codes.

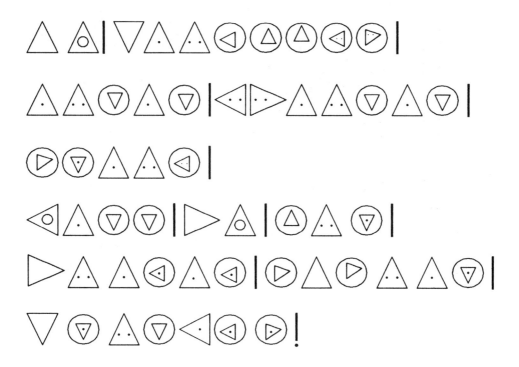

Their minds are also engaged when they are teasing their friends, expressing their sense of humour or using their imagination. In a describe and arrange activity, for example, when one partner has to find out without looking how the other has arranged a set of furniture items on a base picture of a house, it is fairly common for learners to attempt to confuse their friends deliberately by doing something offbeat like putting the fridge in the bathroom...

... Or as one character wrote in a 'note for the electrician', '...*la clef est sous le chien*'!

At an older level, a sixth form class will get quite involved generating a story to 'explain' a picture like the one on the next page.

We probably see the truest form of mental engagement when a class is learning something else through the medium of the language they are learning, say 'doing Science' in Russian.

This kind of mental engagement is one of the ways in which the learners make the language event their own and are not just mouthing others' routines or sentiments. So, the more the better. However, on its own it is often not enough to keep a class working effectively.

PHYSICAL OCCUPATION

Other activities give the learners something physical to do. At one level, speaking is itself a kind of physical involvement in events. Writing is even more obviously occupying. This is often just 'paper and pencil work' of some kind. It might just be copying or, if the class are younger, drawing and colouring. Sometimes the physical activity may be as a result of listening. For example, perhaps pupils have to check items off a list as they hear them or follow a route round a map as they listen to directions (again!). Alternatively, they may be completing a grid with the information they hear. More interestingly, they could be making something by following either spoken or written instructions. They can draw a picture someone else describes. They can make something origami fashion. They can arrange objects or construct something according to instructions. There are also those activities like 'Simon says' which demand rapid physical response. There are others which occupy the learners actively by requiring them to get up and move round the room. One personal favourite is a poster search. For this they have to collect information from a series of 'posters' round the walls. Various forms of class survey or 'sondages' also involve movement around the room. Or there are activities in which they are each given a card and by asking questions (not looking!) have to find the other person in the room who has an identical card to theirs.

Involvement and behaviour

Both of these forms of involvement, that is both physical and mental involvement, contribute positively to the behaviour in an interactive lesson, but each on its own has its limitations which can add to our potential difficulties if they are not taken into account. For example, we need to remind ourselves that excitement with nothing physically active to do can create problems of restlessness. Team games seem like a good idea. But team games which only actively involve one participant from each team at a time and rely on mental involvement alone to hold the attention of the others, often end with rather silly and disruptive arguments about the fairness or otherwise of the scoring system. So we would be looking for ways of retaining the fun but calming things down by giving all the participants something to do. Equally, however physically occupying an activity is, if the work is intellectually and emotionally empty it can lead to boredom. Repeating learnt dialogues in pairs, for example, theoretically occupies everyone and we might expect the activity to be settling. But precisely because they are merely repeating something learnt rather than thinking for themselves or expressing themselves, it doesn't offer the mind or the soul much and the pupils tend to look for other distractions!

On the other hand, look at an activity which you might have expected to make for problems. In the 'poster search' just mentioned, the class moves round the room looking for information on posters on the walls. This is exactly the kind of activity we might be wary of with a difficult class. In fact, it works because it combines mental and physical involvement. It works precisely because they **are** able to move about, talk to each other **and** usually enjoy the challenge of spotting the answer (one fourth year class surprised me by calling it a treasure hunt). They get on with it. There will be noise and normal adolescent shuffle but the class will be working.

If we know all this we can look for ways of adjusting the activities to suit the mood of a lesson.

2   Adjusting the activities

Once you start thinking along these lines you will find that there is often more than one version of an activity which can provide the same linguistic experience while creating a different kind of mood in the room.

Turning a stirrer into a settler

Suppose, for example, you have a list of vocabulary for food and drink which you want to revise. You are still at the stage of getting the class to recognise them. So you decide to do it in some form of lotto. The advantage of this is that it gives a meaningful purpose to the act of repetitive recognition by turning it into a game.

However, although it is a 'pencil and paper' activity which physically occupies the whole class at the same time, it is a highly competitive game that generates excitement and tension. In other words, it can prove something of a stirrer. That is no problem in itself: you maybe want to wake the class up. On the other hand, if for whatever reasons the class needs calming down then you may well want to set up something more settling. At the same time, you don't want to have to abandon this bit of the lesson altogether.

One possibility is to turn it into a simple write-down-the-number-of-the-word-I-say activity. The linguistic practice provided is just the same, but the exercise has a different effect on the mood of the class. It could go like this:

A SETTLING VERSION OF VOCABULARY REVISION

- write your words/stick your flashcards/draw your symbols on the board and number them (you may even find the items are numbered in the textbook for you, in which case you can just work from the book);

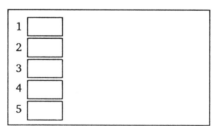

- quickly run through the list saying word or phrase represented by each prompt;

- now say the words/phrases in random order. The class has to write down the numbers in the order you refer to them;

- repeat this as many times as you like, just varying the order. (If you have a lot of words, you may find it works better to do several blocks of five or six at a time rather than all in one go.)

Another possible settling version of the same linguistic activity as lotto is the familiar grid to complete.

If you do not have one ready, you could build up an instant on-the-spot grid on the board. (I personally prefer the class to do this kind of work on scrap paper - then they do not have to spend so long making the grid neat or drawing beautifully. It also avoids filling up their exercise books with meaningless lists of ticks and crosses or numbers etc.) Notice that in spite of the change of outer form, the underlying linguistic task remains the same. Remember too that because you are using this as a settler you need to set it up as swiftly and as uncomplicatedly as possible. One way to do it might be as follows:

ON THE SPOT GRID

- Write the words or initial letters/draw the symbols (keep it simple)/stick five or six prompts across the board, drawing in the vertical lines as you go (the class can start copying as soon as you start; the copying is itself settling).

- Start writing/drawing the first 'down' prompts

	→	←	↑	∃E	📞	✳
B						
H						
C						

- As soon as you can see that the majority of the class has the first 'down' prompt in place, read out your first statement and mark the information on the board grid as they complete theirs. This helps to establish what is happening.

  Pour aller à la banque continuez tout droit puis traversez le pont

- Continue with further statements.*

	→	←	↑	∃E	📞	✳
B		1	2			
H	1	3		2		
C						

Finally, I personally have a standby settler sheet which feels like a test (mega-settler!), but it too makes the same linguistic demands and offers the same linguistic practice as lotto. It also has the advantage that it can be used with any phrase or word, simple or complex, provided you have set up some way of referring to them by numbers.

---

*   It is interesting that words and phrases themselves can contribute to stir/settle. Here, since the intention is to settle the class, we can stick to the rather boringly predictable camping site etc. But on other occasions why not stir things up a bit with a visit to the sewers (a genuine part of the Paris tourist scene), or a stick insect in the list of pets?

NAME _____

a _____	a _____	a _____
b _____	b _____	b _____
c _____	c _____	c _____
d _____	d _____	d _____
e _____	e _____	e _____
f _____	f _____	f _____

a _____	a _____	a _____
b _____	b _____	b _____
c _____	c _____	c _____
d _____	d _____	d _____
e _____	e _____	e _____
f _____	f _____	f _____

I use as many of the boxes as I need to settle the class down initially with series of a write-down-the-number-of-the-one-you-hear. Meanwhile, I decide what I am going to use the rest of the space for! If the going is still tough I will probably use it for another writing activity (maybe an instant grid, maybe copying and label, maybe an exercise from the book), or if things have got better I shall try to use it for something a bit more interesting but still settling.

These particular examples may not appeal to you but what matters is that we each find ways of giving ourselves room for manoeuvre.

A similar kind of adjustment is possible in matters of involvement. Obviously the best activities are those which involve pupils both actively and mentally, for example fitting these strips of jumbled sentence halves together.

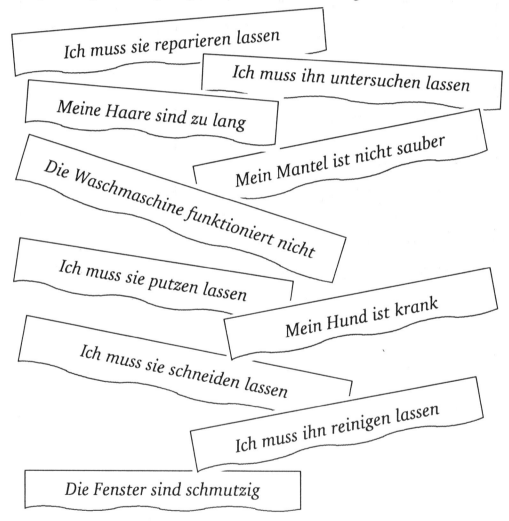

Notice that we have the advantage over the book here in that we can actually give the class pieces of paper to move around. The exercise is much duller on the printed page.

In ways like these you can look for adaptations to increase the mental engagement of mentally involving activities. Writing about these things makes them sound rather heavy-going and complicated. They don't need to be. Here are two examples to give you the general idea.

Increasing actual occupation

There are various versions of the activity which involves the class guessing which phrase/word/object one of their classmates has chosen. In the usual version one pupil selects a flashcard or a word/phrase from a list and the others guess.

¿Vas al banco?
No
¿Vas al correo?
No
¿Vas al supermercado?
Si - si voy

A more complicated version further up the school might go:

'Wenn das Wetter schöner gewesen wäre, hättest du...?'

This can keep even a large class fairly happy for some time because it is fun and it makes them think. Even so, there are disadvantages to the activity in this form. Firstly, any single pupil, even if willing to speak, is not going to have more than one or two chances to do so. Secondly, only one learner is actually speaking at a time. So in this form the activity is mentally engaging but does not involve enough of the class activity. It is therefore a good idea, once it is clear what they have to do, to turn the activity into pair-work in some way. It could go like this:

PAIRED GUESSING

```
1  banco
2  cine
3  supermercado
4  oficina de turismo
5  correo
```

Write/stick/draw prompts on board and number them
Pupil A in each pair writes down the number of the phrase they have chosen

Partner B starts to guess: *Vas al supermercado?* etc

When B has guessed A's choice correctly they change over. B chooses a destination and A has to guess.

In this way you have added actual involvement to the mental involvement of the original. In fact, at a later stage, once they are handling the oral work well and you want to move on to writing, you can turn this into an even more physically involving activity without losing the mental engagement of guessing.

WRITTEN GUESSING

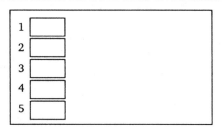

- The prompts are on the board and numbered for reference as before.

  (You may also want to have the written form up. The bright ones don't refer to it, the middle ones will occasionally check, and it provides a constant reminder for those who need it.)

- Both partners choose a phrase. (If they don't trust each other they can write the 'reference number' of the phrase down somewhere out of sight.) Each then has to guess what the other's phrase is.

- Each writes a first guess in the form of a question and they swap papers.

A's paper   B's paper

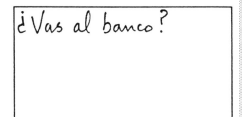

¿Vas al correo?   ¿Vas al banco?

- They indicate on the paper whether their opponent's guess was correct and swap papers back.

¿Vas al correo?   ¿Vas al banco?
¡No!   ¡No!
¿Vas al banco?   ¿Vas al supermercado?
Sí, sí voy.   ¡No!

- They each write the next question and carry on like this until one of them has guessed correctly and scored a point.

- They choose again and start again keeping a score as they go.

So much for increasing actual occupation. In the same way you can increase the mental engagement in something which is effectively occupying but otherwise easily becomes mindless.

Increasing mental engagement

For example, suppose you want a class to get various words connected with shops and shopping into their books. They can, of course, just copy out the list from their textbook or the board. There will be times when that is all you want to do.

But we want the list in their heads as well as in their books. Writing the word just once does not provide much practice and it is possible to copy out lists of words without thinking very much about their meaning. You could increase the mental engagement and the chances of effective learning by asking the class to list their words in categories like this:

---

im Wohnzimmer   **im Schlafzimmer**

der Tisch
der Stuhl
die Lampe
der Schrank
das Fernsehen

in der Küche   **im Badezimmer**

der Tisch
der Stuhl
die Lampe

                                                          etc

---

If this idea appeals to you, there are several ways you can turn it into a much fuller version. Here is one:

LISTING

- Ask the class to work in pairs to make a rough list of any weather phrases they know - they can approximate if they don't know how to spell them. Give them a couple of minutes to do this.

- On one side of the board or on the OHP collect together the phrases they have thought of. (This is your chance to spell their rough or half-remembered versions correctly. At this stage I prefer just to let them tell me, in however rough and ready form, what they have thought of. I do not ask them to spell the phrases. After all, if they can already produce all these in correct spelling there is no need to do the activity!)

```
es schneit
es regnet
es ist kalt
die Sonne scheint
es friert
es ist nebelig
es ist windig
es ist warm
es ist bewölkt
```

- When you have a reasonable list collected on the board or the OHP, read them through quickly with the class so they are reminded of the sound before they write them.

- Next write the four seasons up as headings

```
es schneit
es regnet          Winter      Sommer
es ist kalt
die Sonne scheint
es friert
es ist nebelig     Frühling    Herbst
es ist windig
es ist warm
es ist bewölkt
```

- Read out one of the phrases and allocate it to a season. (Choose one which will make it clear that things can come in more than one category.)

```
es schneit
es regnet          Winter          Sommer
es ist kalt        es regnet        die Sonne
die Sonne scheint  es ist kalt          scheint
es friert                           es ist warm
es ist nebelig
es ist windig      Frühling         Herbst
es ist warm        es regnet        es regnet
es ist bewölkt
```

- Do a couple of examples like this and then set the class to write the column headings in their own books and to make the lists according to what they think is appropriate.

There are plenty of categories and items you can use this technique with, e.g. shops and purchases, weather and clothes, days of the week and school subjects, rooms and furniture and so on. The only thing to remember is that you want to provide personal choice but you also want the items to come up several times (or as one of my pupils said perceptively though not eloquently to his neighbour 'I've just written *es* bloody *regnet* four times!').

So what!

To say all this may seem to be labouring the point and stating the obvious. It may well be obvious, but even so it is not uncommon for the start of a long lesson or the whole of a short lesson to follow a pattern something like this:

AIM: TO PRACTISE REQUEST + FOOD		
Time	**Activity**	**Comment**
5 mins	General questions routine	Oral, one pupil at a time - STIR
5 mins	Revision of food vocabulary flashcards and repetition	Oral, little occupation or mental involvement, therefore STIR
5 mins	Practise request and food with exercise p 120	Oral, little occupation or mental involvement, therefore STIR
5 mins	Practise reading dialogue p121	Oral/reading, a bit more occupation but still little mental involvement, therefore STIR
10 mins	In pairs practise dialogue p 121 ready for acting out	

I have exaggerated this slightly to make the point, but set out in this way it becomes clear that the first twenty minutes or so of a lesson like this would offer little to settle or to occupy the bulk of the class so that by the time the teacher came to set up the interactive work the class would at best be probably only partly attentive and willing. If this were the beginning of a double period, the situation could become even more uncomfortable. Even with a fairly ordinary class and a short single period the lesson as it stands could prove quite a handful. There would certainly be problems ahead if the class contained a sizeable proportion of the uncommitted or easily distracted.

Obviously some teachers can assert control but why set up a lesson so that we constantly have to? Our understanding of stir/settle and involvement doesn't just give us flexibility in the form of the activities themselves, it also gives us flexibility in respect of the way in which we can sequence activities and have some control over the general mood of the lesson.

3   Adjusting the sequence of activities

There are perhaps three main ways we can usefully adjust lessons taking stir/settle and the contributory factor of involvement into account.

i)   We can start lessons in such a way as to calm a class down.

ii) We can try to make sure that lively work starts from and returns to a relatively calm base.

iii) We are in a better position to handle those lessons which are longer than we would have ideally chosen.

Starting lessons calmly

Unless you have the kind of class you have to kick-start in order to achieve anything at all, it helps to begin most lessons with something calming. We've all got ways of settling classes down right at the beginning before we start work. But there is no point in throwing away that hard-won attention by then making the first twenty minutes of activities stirring or not very involving. So one technique is quite deliberately to insert settlers at the beginning of the lesson. In fact, if you find you can't get quiet by demanding it or if you prefer a more indirect control, then these activities will often help slide a class into a calm mood.

What settlers people use are a matter of personal preference. Here are three possibilities. The first is based on writing, the second on listening and the third on reading. They are all quite deliberately **very** basic. If they take time to set up or if they are complicated they no longer work as settlers.

Suggestion 1.	Get the class to copy a brief list of words/phrases/structures which you are going to focus on later.
Suggestion 2.	Try the write-down-the-number-of-the-one-I-say activity set out on page 10.
Suggestion 3.	Get the class to turn to the page in the book which you are going to use later. Read out in random order a collection of key words/phrases/structures which occur in the text. The class have to track them down in the text and copy them out.

These settling tasks may be very basic but they are not pointless. They can be a way to highlight the focus of the lesson or to ease the way into a rather large chunk of text.

Remember too that these settlers can be combined to provide a more prolonged calming start on those occasions when the class have come into the room with their hair standing up on end. This leads us on to the question of longer sequences of activities and particularly those leading up to and following interactive work of some kind.

Providing a calm context for lively work

We can't ask young people to have fun, move about, talk to each other etc and then be surprised and annoyed if they get noisy and excited.

'You are to practise this dialogue in pairs - and there is to be no talking!'

So, if we know that something lively is coming up, we can sandwich it between activities which are basically calming. For example, suppose you are planning to get the class to learn some dialogues, practise them in pairs and then 'act' them out in front of the others. For reasons already discussed, the practising of the dialogues often won't hold their attention for long enough for them to learn the dialogues! And because watching or listening to your mates isn't very involving, many classes are not very good at keeping quiet while others are doing their bit. So you can set up the mood more calmly by making sure that the pair-work follows and is followed by settlers rather than stirrers. For example:

- in pairs, sort out the dialogue on strips of paper into the right sequence (or a possible sequence; no reason why everyone should have to do your thing);

- practise it in pairs and do some acting out;

- each pair copies up its chosen version.

For more difficult situations you can make this interweaving of stir and settle more frequent. For example, a more extreme version might then look like this:

- paired rehearsing of dialogues as planned;

- switch to a sort-the-strips-into-order activity based on the dialogue;

- bit more dialogue repeating;

- then some acting out as planned;

- then copy out the strip dialogue they have previously sorted out;

- then back to a couple more acting out;
  If you still want to continue with the dialogue but the pronunciation is going to pot, you can combine a reminder of what it sounds like with a settler in the form of some version of write-down-the-number-of-the-one-you-hear.

- final return to acting out dialogues.

This kind of interweaving of stir and settle is also what makes long lessons much more manageable.

Pacing long lessons

We seem at times to have got into the way of thinking of good language teaching as resembling some kind of song and dance routine. 'Superteach' bounds confidently into the classroom with a song at the ready, paper bag puppets in the left hand, flashcards in the right, a stick of chalk between the teeth and a chin operated tape-recorder slung round the neck!

'Right! Calm down!'

We are asking the impossible of ourselves if we try to teach at maximum pitch all the time. More importantly, we are letting the learners down. They need peace and quiet in their lives as well as stimulation and excitement. Schools may be one of the few remaining places where some of them have a chance of finding it. We cannot moan about their inability to concentrate if we subject them to a constant barrage of high voltage activities. Besides, our language lesson is only one in their day's programme. So we owe them - and need for our own sakes - periods of calm in amongst the bursts of activity.

To oversimplify again, you can use the stir/settle concept to create a pattern a bit like this:

for a basically lively class　　　　　**for a basically stodgy class**

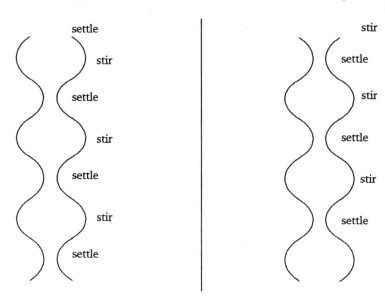

This kind of planning isn't a long and complicated process. Once you've decided to think in this way it becomes almost instinctive. It also works! By varying the mood in this way through the choice and sequence of activities we have more chance of making sure that a long lesson does not build up unstoppably to a pitch of unacceptable behaviour or slide down into a slough of dullness.

It may help to summarise all these points if we return to the lesson on requests + food on page 20. Here is an alternative version which puts some of the suggestions in this book into practice.

AIM: TO PRACTISE REQUEST + FOOD	COMMENT

Time	Activity	
15	On arrival, class to copy food list onto rough paper/rough books/back of books	Simultaneously occupying,-SETTLER
	With flashcards numbered on board do 'write down the number of the one you hear'.	Simultaneously occupying with a little more mental engagement, but still SETTLING
	(approx 3 times + vary it to true/false, i.e. 1, *des frites - vrai? faux?*)	
10	Practise question with 'guess what I've got on my flashcard'.	STIR, mentally engaging
	Paired 'guess what I've got on my flashcard'.	STIR, mentally engaging + simultaneously **occupying**
	Write *vous désirez* on board	
5	'Dictation', i.e. recognition and copying of request + food (front of books as a record).	RESETTLE with simultaneous occupation (writing) + mental engagement in order to remind of sound and settle before STIR
	In pairs, practise dialogue page 121 ready for acting out.	

27

Final comments

1. It is very tempting with difficult classes to set up lessons which are all settlers. (Or as one 11-year-old once assured me on transferring to secondary school *'I don't do French ... I draw'*.) That defeats the purpose of the exercise which is to calm things down sometimes, so that at other times you can do more lively things without events getting out of hand.

2. This isn't just a negative mechanism for dealing with energetic classes, though the focus in this particular book has been on control. The approach is just as valid as a way of making sure that we wake up our more plodding classes.

3. Finally, there are conventions about language teaching which imply that some activities are inherently GOOD and others are inherently BAD. For example, teachers can be made to feel very guilty about asking their class to copy or getting them to write words before they have said them. I am not dismissing those conventions. They are based on helpful pedagogic insights. I am arguing, however, that no single activity or sequence of activities is GOOD if it causes problems in terms of the human reactions to the lessons. A flower is a weed if there are too many of them or they are in the wrong place. For our own sanity and the sake of our classes we have to take people as well as more theoretical language pedagogy into account.